FRANCHISING IN TAIWAN 2014

Legal and Business Considerations

AF873383

KENDAL H. TYRE, JR., EXECUTIVE EDITOR
DIANA VILMENAY-HAMMOND, MANAGING EDITOR
PIERCE HAESUNG HAN, ASSISTANT EDITOR

LEXNOIR FOUNDATION

SECOND QUARTER 2014

LexNoir Foundation is the charitable, educational arm of LexNoir, an international network of lawyers connecting the African Diaspora.

This publication, *Franchising in Taiwan 2014: Legal and Business Considerations*, contains excerpts from *Franchising in Asia 2014: Legal and Business Considerations*. Both works are published by LexNoir Foundation and reflect the points of view of the authors and editors as of the date of publication and do not necessarily represent the opinions, interpretations, or positions of the law firms or organizations with which they are affiliated, nor the opinions, interpretations or positions of LexNoir Foundation or LexNoir.

Nothing contained in this book is to be considered as the rendering of legal advice, either generally or in connection with any specific issues or case. Readers are responsible for obtaining advice from their own legal counsel or other professional. This book, any forms and agreements or other information herein are intended for educational and informational purposes only.

© 2014 LexNoir Foundation. All rights reserved.

www.lexnoir.org

Franchising in Taiwan

Patricia Ginsberg
Pamir Law Group

Bibliography of International Franchise Resources

Kendal H. Tyre, Jr., Diana Vilmenay-Hammond, Pierce Haesung Han and Keri McWilliams
Nixon Peabody LLP

Acknowledgment

This book could not have been written without the hard work and dedication of each of the contributing authors and editors. Thank you.

We would like to acknowledge and extend our heartfelt gratitude to Maria Stallings of the Washington, D.C. office of Nixon Peabody LLP for her invaluable assistance in revising, proofing, and editing this publication.

About the Editors and Authors

Kendal H. Tyre, Jr. – Kendal is a partner in the Washington, D.C. office of Nixon Peabody LLP. He handles domestic and cross-border transactions, including mergers and acquisitions, joint ventures, strategic alliances, licensing, and franchise matters.

In his franchise and licensing practice, Kendal counsels domestic and international franchisors, franchisees, licensors, licensees and distributors regarding U.S. state and federal franchise laws as well as foreign franchise legislation in a variety of jurisdictions. Kendal drafts and provides advice with regard to franchise and license agreements, disclosure documents and area development agreements and has extensive experience drafting and negotiating a variety of other commercial agreements. His client base spans the United States and foreign countries, including South Africa, Kenya, and the United Kingdom.

Kendal is a frequent contributor to franchise publications and a frequent speaker at franchise programs held by the American Bar Association Forum on Franchising and the International Franchise Association.

Kendal is co-chair of the firm's Diversity Action Committee and its Africa Group. Kendal is also the executive director of LexNoir Foundation.

E-mail address: ktyre@nixonpeabody.com

Diana Vilmenay-Hammond – Diana is an attorney in the Washington, D.C. office of Nixon Peabody LLP. She is a member of the firm's Franchise & Distribution team.

In her franchise practice, Diana works with domestic and international franchisors on transactional and litigation matters. Specifically, she counsels franchisor clients regarding state and federal franchise laws, disclosure and registration obligations. Diana drafts and negotiates various commercial agreements, including international franchise and development agreements.

Diana has co-authored numerous articles on franchising and frequently co-hosted the Nixon Peabody franchise law webinar series. Topics have included:

- "Franchise Case Law Round-Up: Implications for Your Franchise;"
- "Social Media Part II: Best Practices in Protecting Your Brand in the New Media;" and
- "The Awuah Case: Bellwether or Outlier."

Diana received her J.D. from Howard University School of Law and her B.A. from Georgetown University. She is a member of the American Bar Association (Forum on Franchising).

E-mail address: dvilmenay@nixonpeabody.com

Pierce Haesung Han – Pierce is an associate in Nixon Peabody's Global Business & Transactions group. Pierce focuses his practice on three main areas, assisting clients with a variety of complex business transactions.

- Mergers & Acquisitions: Providing assistance to both public and private clients with various mergers and acquisitions, performing due diligence, drafting and negotiating transaction documents, and facilitating closing and post-closing mechanics.
- International Commercial Transactions: Drafting and negotiating a variety of commercial agreements,

including international franchise and development agreements, license agreements, and purchase and sale agreements.

- Federal Securities Law Matters: Assisting public and private clients regarding federal securities laws and stock exchange rules relating to corporate governance and disclosure.

Pierce serves as the Secretary of the Asian Pacific Bar Association Educational Fund (an affiliate of the Asian Pacific American Bar Association of the Greater Washington, D.C. Area).

Pierce received his J.D. from Georgetown University Law Center and his B.A. from Case Western Reserve University. He is admitted to practice in the State of New York and the District of Columbia.

E-mail address: phan@nixonpeabody.com

Keri McWilliams – Keri is an associate in the Franchise & Distribution team of Nixon Peabody LLP. Keri works with clients on a number of franchising issues, including obtaining and maintaining franchise registrations in various states, responding to state inquiries regarding trade practices, ongoing compliance with state and federal regulations, and updating franchise disclosure documents. She also handles franchise sales counseling and franchise system issues.

Keri is a member of the American Bar Association's Forum on Franchising, and the Federal and Minnesota State bar associations. She is also a member of Minnesota Women Lawyers and the Minnesota Association of Black Lawyers, and a volunteer in the Volunteer Lawyers Network.

Keri received her J.D. from Georgetown University Law Center and her B.F.A. from Washington University. She is admitted to practice in the District of Columbia and Minnesota.

E-mail address: kmcwilliams@nixonpeabody.com

Patrica Ginsberg – Patricia is a partner based in Pamir Law Group's Taipei office. With an international law and business foundation and multi-lingual proficiencies, Patricia has focused her practice on international corporate and commercial transactions for multinational and local companies. She has represented and counseled clients investing from U.S. and Europe into Asia and also in the reverse direction. In addition, she has assisted Asian companies in projects within the Asian region.

Her experiences include assisting clients in joint ventures, mergers & acquisitions, employments matters, structured management buyouts, technology licensing for technology-based clients, alternative dispute resolution, and assisting both lenders and borrowers in aircraft leasing and ship financings. While living in North America, Asia and also Europe, Patricia gained valuable insights into issues faced by global businesses today. Her background provides her with keen awareness of Eastern and Western customs, often positioning her to bridge cultural and business gaps during legal/business negotiations and planning.

Patricia received her B.A. from Wellesley College in 1995. She earned both her J.D. and Master's degree from Washington University in St. Louis in 1998, where she was the recipient of the National Order of Barristers. She also received her M.B.A. from McGill University in 2004.

E-mail address: pginsberg@pamirlaw.com

About the Book

Franchising in Taiwan 2014: Legal and Business Considerations contains excerpts from the larger work *Franchising in Asia 2014: Legal and Business Considerations*. Both books serve as practical, succinct, easy-to-use reference tools for lawyers, business people and academics to use in navigating the laws and business issues impacting franchise arrangements in Asia.

This book provides an overview of the franchise industry in Taiwan and addresses the typical legal issues confronted when expanding a franchise system in Taiwan. The larger work, *Franchising in Asia 2014: Legal and Business Considerations*, covers those laws governing franchising in several other Asian countries.

In both books, an author, who is a legal expert in the designated jurisdiction, addresses the basic questions that a franchise lawyer would need to know to competently represent a client in expanding their franchise system to that country.

Each country chapter organizes a discussion of that country's laws under various headings and in a uniform format. Topics were sent to each country's author in the form of a questionnaire, and each author drafted responses to the questions presented. A general overview relating to the political and economic history of the country at the beginning of each chapter provides an initial context for the regulatory framework.[1]

---

1 The source of information for these sections is the Central Intelligence Agency, https://www.cia.gov/library/publications/the-world-factbook/ (last visited May 15, 2014).

Apart from an overview of the legal framework for franchising, each book contains other articles and resources that should prove useful to those in the franchise industry.

The authors for each chapter are listed at the beginning of a chapter and their biographical information is listed in the previous section, *About the Editors and Authors*.

Readers should always consult with local counsel in the relevant jurisdiction instead of relying solely on the information contained in this book. The laws governing franchising are evolving and local counsel in Taiwan are best positioned to provide timely, relevant advice applying the current law to the particular facts of a case.

Franchising in Taiwan

Patricia Ginsberg
Pamir Law Group
Taipei, Taiwan

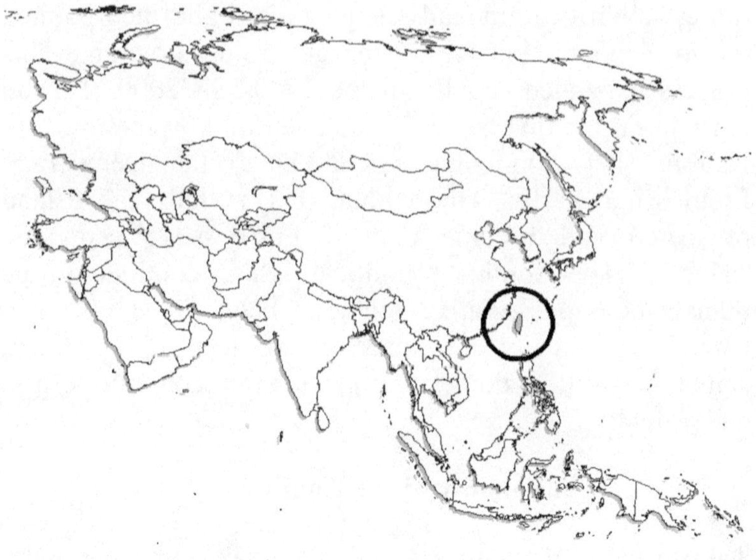

Taiwan

I. Introduction

A. Historical Background of the Country

Taiwan came under Chinese Nationalist control after World War II. Following the communist victory on the mainland in 1949, 2 million Nationalists fled to Taiwan and established a government using the 1947 constitution drawn up for all of China. Beginning in the 1950s, the ruling authorities gradually democratized and incorporated the local population within the governing structure. This process expanded rapidly in the 1980s. In 2000, Taiwan underwent its first peaceful transfer of power from the Nationalist (Kuomintang or KMT) to the Democratic Progressive Party. Throughout this period, the island prospered and became one of East Asia's economic "Tigers." The dominant political issues continue to be management of sensitive relations between Taiwan and China—specifically the question of Taiwan's eventual status—as well as domestic priorities for economic reform and growth.

B. Economy of the Country

Taiwan has a dynamic capitalist economy with gradually decreasing government guidance of investment and foreign trade. Exports, led by electronics, machinery, and petrochemicals have provided the primary impetus for economic development. This heavy dependence on exports exposes the economy to fluctuations in world demand.

Free trade agreements have proliferated in East Asia over the past several years, and following the landmark Economic Cooperation Framework Agreement (ECFA) signed with China in June 2010, Taiwan in July 2013 signed a free trade deal with New Zealand—Taipei's first-ever with a country with which it does not maintain diplomatic relations—and in November inked a trade pact with Singapore. Negotiations continue on follow-on components of ECFA regarding trade in goods and a dispute resolution mechanism; a trade in services agreement is under review in the legislature.

The island runs a large overall trade surplus largely because of its surplus with China, and its foreign reserves are the world's sixth largest, behind China, Japan, Saudi Arabia, Russia, and Switzerland. In 2006 China overtook the U.S. to become Taiwan's second-largest source of imports after Japan. China is also the island's number one destination for foreign direct investment. Taiwan since 2009 has gradually loosened rules governing Chinese investment on the island, and has also secured greater market access for its investors in the mainland. In August 2012, Taiwan Central Bank signed a memorandum of understanding on cross-Strait currency settlement with its Chinese counterpart. The MOU allows for the direct settlement of Chinese RMB and the New Taiwan dollar across the Strait, which could help develop Taiwan into a local RMB hub. Closer economic links with the mainland bring greater opportunities for the Taiwan economy, but also poses new challenges as the island becomes more economically dependent on China while political differences remain unresolved.

C. Franchise Legal Overview

In Taiwan, franchise activities are not regulated by any franchise specific legislation. However, the *Taiwan Fair Trade Act* ("Act") addresses matters concerning fair trade and competition and thus the Act applies to franchise transactions. The Taiwan Fair Trade Commission ("TFTC") has promulgated guidelines concerning franchising. In 1999, the TFTC issued the "*Guidelines on the Disclosure of Information by Franchisors*" (renamed as the "*Fair Trade Commission Disposal Directions (Policy*

Statements) on the Business Practices of Franchisors")[2] ("Guidelines"). The Guidelines are designed to promote fair dealing and prevent franchisors from concealing important information during solicitation of potential franchisees.

II. Regulatory Requirements

A. Pre-sale Disclosure

Please describe any pre-sale franchise disclosure or similar requirements that may apply to franchise transactions.

Under the Guidelines, a franchisor must disclose material information in writing to a prospective franchisee at least ten days before entering into a franchise agreement (or within a reasonable period of time, depending on the specifics of a case). The Guidelines stipulate that material information includes, but is not limited to, the following items:

1. expenses before operation such as any applicable franchise fee[s], training charges, expenses for product purchases and capital equipment, etc. (each such item, its corresponding amount and total estimate must be clearly listed);

2. expenses during operation such as license fee calculation and payment, management instruction fees, products and raw material costs (each such item, its corresponding amount and total estimate must be clearly listed);

---

2 The Guidelines were amended on November 20, 2003, December 24, 2008, May 18, 2011 and February 8, 2012.

3. the trademark right, patent and copyright involved, and their contents, validity periods, extent of authorization and restrictive conditions;

4. management assistance, training, and instruction;

5. plans for setting up other franchisees under the same franchise system in the franchisee's operating area;

6. the total number and location of franchisees under the same franchise system in the same county or city, and the statistics (ratio) of contract cancellation and termination in the previous year;

7. restrictions regarding the franchise relationship during the contract period, including:

    a. terms concerning supply of products, raw materials, capital equipment, etc. (specifications and names of suppliers or contractors);

    b. items and quantities of products or raw materials to be purchased; and

    c. any other restrictions with regard to the franchise relationship; and

8. conditions on amendment and termination.

In addition to the advance disclosure of material information, the franchise agreement itself must be provided to a prospective franchisee at least five days prior to signing to enable the prospective franchisee an opportunity to review the agreement. The parties should execute the agreement in duplicate, with one original held by the franchisee.

B. Government Approvals, Registrations, Filing Requirements.

Please describe any necessary government approvals, registrations, or filing requirements that may apply to franchise transactions.

With the exception of the requirements stipulated in the Guidelines described above, it is not necessary to have governmental approvals or registrations before parties enter into a franchise arrangement. Furthermore, there is no registration or filing requirements that apply once the parties have signed the franchise agreement and entered into the franchise relationship. Please note, however, where it is necessary to convert Taiwanese currency to the relevant foreign currency, franchise fee payments made overseas may be subject to additional reporting requirements (See Section III).

C. Limits on Fees and Typical Term of Franchise Agreement

Please describe any limits upon the nature and extent of fees and the term of a typical franchise agreement.

In general, franchisors and franchisees are free to agree on the relevant fees and the conditions of their transaction. There are no upper or lower limits on the amount of fees that a franchisor charges its franchisee. Although parties are free to agree on the terms and conditions, a franchisor should not abuse its position and the dependence of its franchisees. The Guidelines identify several prohibited activities that violate fair trade and dealings under the Act:

Taiwan

1. Differentiated Treatment

A franchisor would be deemed to violate Article 19(2) of the Act if the franchisor engages in differentiated treatment regarding price, trading terms or transactions with various franchisees or other businesses at the same competition level without justifiable reasons and such conduct leads to competition restriction or impediment of fair competition.

2. Improper Restrictions on Franchisees

In order to protect their intellectual property rights, brand image and interests, or the overall business reputation of the franchise system, franchisors may impose necessary but reasonable restrictions. Improper and unreasonable restrictions leading to competition restriction or impediment of fair competition violate Article 19(6) of the Act. Examples of such illegal conduct include, but are not limited to, the following:

a. Tie-In Sales

Without justifiable reasons, a franchisor demands its franchisee to buy additional different product(s) when the franchisee is purchasing certain products.

b. Trading Counterpart Restriction

Without justifiable reasons, a franchisor imposes restrictions on its franchisee with regard to product sales, capital equipment, raw materials, and furnishing of work, such as the mandatory engagement of suppliers or contractors designated by the franchisor. Such conduct will most likely be regarded as leading to competition restriction or to the impediment of fair competition. The franchisor, however, may make recommendations so long as the selection of suppliers or contractors is not mandatory.

c. Compulsory Purchase Amounts

Without justifiable reasons, a franchisor demands its franchisee to purchase specific quantities of products or raw materials and prohibits their return and such quantities exceed what the franchisee is able to sell within a reasonable number of business days or surpass the stock quantities a franchisee requires. Such conduct will most likely be regarded as leading to competition restriction or to the impediment of fair competition.

III. Currency

If all payments under a franchise agreement must be made in immediately available U.S. Dollars, please advise as to any restrictions, reporting requirements, or regulations concerning the exchange, repatriation or remittance of U.S. Dollars.

Payments under a franchise agreement do not need to be denominated in U.S. Dollars. Under the "*Regulations Governing the Declaration of Foreign Exchange Receipts and Disbursements or Transaction,*"[3] if an amount wired overseas is greater than Five Hundred Thousand New Taiwan Dollars (NT$500,000, roughly US$17,241 at an exchange rate of US$1:NT$29), then the local bank must

3 Promulgated on August 30, 1995, and amended on December 27, 1995, June 11, 1997, December 31, 2001, March 30, 2002, April 30, 2003, and June 01, 2010.

report to the Central Bank of the Republic of China (Taiwan) ("Central Bank") regarding the purpose of the remittance. If a single remittance by a company is at or over One Million United States Dollars (US$1,000,000), then besides reporting to the Central Bank, one would need to submit the "transaction documents" such as the franchise agreement. For an entity (as opposed to a natural person), the annual remittance for an entire year should not be greater than Fifty Million United States Dollars (US$50,000,000) in the aggregate. If the remittance will exceed such maximum figure, prior approval of the Central Bank is required.

IV. Taxes, Tariffs and Duties

Please do not provide any in-depth comments on tax structuring. However, please provide your general comments on the typical amount of withholding tax that would apply and whether a "gross-up" provision contained in a franchise agreement would be enforceable in your country.

Absent tax treaties, the withholding tax levied on a franchisee's payment made to a foreign franchisor with no permanent existence in Taiwan is twenty percent (20%). "Gross up" provisions are enforceable in Taiwan.

Taiwan is a signatory of double taxation treaties with the following countries: Australia, Belgium, Denmark, Gambia, Indonesia, Macedonia, Malaysia, New Zealand, Senegal, Singapore, South Africa, Swaziland, Sweden, the Netherlands, United Kingdom, Vietnam, India, Israel, Thailand, France, Germany, Hungary, Slovakia and Paraguay. Additionally, Taiwan has double taxation agreements for the shipping or air transport industry with: Canada, the European Union, Germany, Israel, Japan,

Korea, Luxembourg, Macau, the Netherlands, Norway, Sweden, Thailand and the United States.

V. Trademarks

Please advise us as to whether there are any special requirements for granting a valid trademark license, including the use of a registered user agreement or a short trademark license agreement and any required filing of such an agreement with the trademark authorities.

The agency in charge of intellectual property in Taiwan is the Intellectual Property Office of the Ministry of Economic Affairs ("Taiwan Intellectual Property Office"). There are no special requirements for granting a valid trademark license. The Taiwan Intellectual Property Office does not require users to register or file their license agreement. Mutual consent alone will suffice. A franchisor can still register the trademark license with the Taiwan Intellectual Property Office. By doing this, the trademark license registration can act as a defense against certain types of third party claims. For this reason, it is recommended that franchisors and franchisees apply to the Registrar Office at the Taiwan Intellectual Property Office to record the license.

A franchisor who has not registered its trademark in Taiwan is recommended to do so since Taiwan Trademark Law applies the "first to file" principle and affords protection to a trademark upon registration. It is, therefore, important to file trademark application(s) on the earliest possible date. A foreign individual or entity must appoint an agent in Taiwan to apply for the registration of a mark on its behalf to the Taiwan Intellectual Property Office.

Priority can be claimed for a trademark application if it is filed within six months from the date of the first registration application of the same trademark in a country that has a treaty or agreement with Taiwan concerning reciprocal trademark protection. Taiwan became a member of the World Trade Organization ("WTO") on January 1, 2002; thus, priority can be claimed by any applicant of any other WTO member state.

In Taiwan, registered marks are designated as "trademarks," regardless of whether they cover goods or services. One application can cover one mark for goods or services in one or more class(es). However, a multi-class application will not be permitted if the priority date for one class is from one country and the priority date for another class is from a different country. In that case, separate applications must be made.

In terms of timing, the Taiwan Intellectual Property Office normally takes about eight to ten months to process a trademark application once all required supporting documents have been properly submitted. After the application is approved, an approval letter will be sent to the applicant. Registration fees must be paid within two months from the date the approval letter is received. After the payment of registration fees, the Taiwan Intellectual Property Office will publish the mark as a registered trademark in the *Government Gazette*. The applicant will obtain the trademark rights and certificate as of the publication date. Anyone may file an opposition to the registration within three months from the publication date. Therefore, although the certificate is given, the trademark rights are not fully valid until three months after the publication and as long as no objections by third parties are made.

VI. Restrictions on Transfer

Please advise as to whether there are any restrictions (1) on a franchisor to restrict transfers by a master franchisee, any interest in a master franchisee, or the assets of the master franchisee or (2) the ability of a master franchisee to control and/or restrict transfers of a subfranchisee's rights under a master franchise agreement, an interest in the subfranchisee, or the assets of the subfranchisee.

Under Taiwanese laws, there is no specific law regulating franchise businesses. The franchisor-franchisee relationship is subject to the franchise agreement itself under general contract rules and principles, which are covered by the Civil Code of Taiwan ("Civil Code"). There are no restrictions (1) on a franchisor to restrict transfers by a master franchisee, any interest in a master franchisee, or the assets of the master franchisee or (2) the ability of a master franchisee to control and/or restrict transfers of a subfranchisee's rights under a master franchise agreement, an interest in the subfranchisee, or the assets of the subfranchisee. Terms and conditions should be clearly stated in the franchise agreement, should be conscionable and should not violate public order or morale and cannot violate fair and reasonable trading order.

VII. Termination

Please advise us as to any laws relating to termination in your country, such as agency laws, required indemnity provisions, notice or "good cause" requirements, or other laws affecting termination of a franchise agreement. Please describe.

As mentioned above, Taiwan does not have specific laws regulating franchise businesses. The franchisor-franchisee relationship is subject to the franchise agreement itself under general contract rules and principles, which are covered by the Civil Code. There are no restrictions or requirements concerning indemnity provisions or termination for good cause. The parties are free to agree on terms and conditions of their franchise relationship; provided however, that the terms should be conscionable and should not violate public order or morale. Terms and conditions regarding termination should be clearly stated in the franchise agreement and cannot violate fair and reasonable trading order.

VIII. Governing Law, Jurisdiction and Dispute Resolution

A. Choice of Law of Foreign Jurisdiction

Please confirm whether the choice of law of a foreign jurisdiction would likely to be upheld under the law of the country, except for certain matters such as trademarks, bankruptcy and competition matters, which we assume would be governed by the law in your country.

Under Taiwan's conflict of laws principles, contracting parties are free to determine the governing law for their agreement, and their selection will be respected. If the parties do not agree on the governing law, courts in Taiwan will apply the law with the greatest connection to the case in accordance with the type of dispute. For instance, if the dispute concerns a debt relation (e.g., the franchisee owes the franchisor royalties), then the location where the debtor's actions took place is assumed to be the greatest connection to such type of cases.

B. International Arbitration Dispute Resolution

Taiwan

Please confirm that a court in your country would honor an election of international arbitration dispute resolution, and therefore refuse to hear any disputes arising under a franchise agreement.

Under Taiwanese law, contracting parties are free to determine their dispute resolution method, including their selection to pursue arbitration instead of court litigation. The parties may also agree to select foreign arbitration instead of domestic arbitration. According to the *Arbitration Act of Taiwan*, if a party to an arbitration agreement files a lawsuit contrary to the arbitration agreement, the adverse party has the right to petition the court to suspend the lawsuit. The court would then order the parties to submit to arbitration. In such cases, if the party fails to submit to arbitration, the court will dismiss the legal action.

Taiwan is not a party to the *Convention on the Recognition and Enforcement of Foreign Arbitral Awards* (the "New York Convention") because it is not a member of the United Nations. Despite not being a signatory to the New York Convention, foreign arbitral awards can nevertheless be recognized and enforced in Taiwan. The *Arbitration Act in Taiwan* is based on the *UNCITRAL Model Law of 1985* ("UNCITRAL Law"), and it applies to both domestic and international arbitrations. Except on narrow grounds relating to the lack of jurisdiction, the improper constitution of the tribunal, serious procedural irregularity, or an award countering public policy, countries such as Taiwan that have adopted UNCITRAL Law will usually recognize and enforce foreign arbitral awards. In the case of Taiwan, the courts do, however, have the additional discretion to refuse recognition if the country where the award was made or under whose law the award was issued, refuses to recognize Taiwanese arbitral awards. The party wishing to enforce a foreign award in Taiwan should first apply to a Taiwanese court for recognition. The application should include the original arbitration agreement together with the original arbitral award document (if any of the originals are not available, then an authenticated copy is required). These documents submitted to the court must be translated into Chinese if they are in a foreign language and must be legalized by the Taiwanese embassy or its functional equivalent located at the applicable jurisdiction. The petitioner must comply with these formalities to prevent the application from being dismissed. An award would be recognized and enforced unless the court determines that the award contravenes public order or good morals of Taiwan or if the dispute could not be arbitrated under the laws of Taiwan or pursuant to any of the narrow grounds stated above. Even if such narrow grounds do not exist, the court may still, at its discretion, dismiss an application for the award recognition if the country where the arbitral award is made or whose laws govern the arbitral award does not recognize arbitral awards from Taiwan. After recognition by the court, the petitioner should then apply to the Civil Execution Department of the relevant District Court for enforcement of the award. An execution fee for enforcement would be determined and must then be paid.

IX. Non-Competition Provisions

If the franchise agreement prohibits the franchisee from engaging in certain competitive activities during the term of the agreement, and for a 12-month period after the termination or expiration of the agreement, please comment on the enforceability of non-competition covenants in your country.

To protect the intellectual property and business interests of the franchisor, a non-competition clause with a reasonable non-compete period is allowed under Taiwanese law. There is no black letter law stipulating the exact period a non-compete would be considered reasonable or permissible; however, in practice, a period of up to two years after the termination or expiration of the agreement will usually be enforceable.

X. Language Requirements

Does the law in your country require that a franchise agreement be translated into the local language in order to be enforceable between the parties?

Taiwan does not require that a franchise agreement be in the Chinese language to be valid and enforceable between the parties. However, in the event of a dispute presented to Taiwanese courts, all evidence and documents, including the franchise agreement, would need to be translated into Chinese. Should the case be arbitrated, the parties are free to decide the language in which the arbitration is to be conducted as well as the language of the evidentiary documents.

XI. Other Significant Matters

Please advise as to whether there are any significant matters not addressed above of which a franchisor should be aware in connection with its entering into a franchise agreement in your country.

Taiwan has a few franchise associations, which are not affiliated with the government. Their names and contact details are provided below:

Taiwan Chain Stores and Franchise Association
4F, No. 180, Nanking E. Road,
Section 4, Taipei 105, Taiwan
TEL: 886-2-2579-6262 FAX: 886-2-2579-1176
http://www.tcfa.org.tw/

Taiwan

Association of Chain and Franchise Promotion, Taiwan
7F., No.82, Sec. 1, Zhongshan N. Rd.,
Zhongshan Dist., Taipei City 104, Taiwan
TEL: 886-2-2523-5118 FAX: 886-2-2523-0229
http://www.franchise.org.tw/about_e.php

Taiwan

Bibliography of International Franchise Resources

Kendal H. Tyre, Jr., Diana Vilmenay-Hammond, Pierce Haesung Han and Keri McWilliams
Nixon Peabody LLP
Washington, D.C.

I. General International Resources

Mark Abell, Gary R. Duvall, and Andrea Oricchio Kirsh, *International Franchise Legislation* B1, ABA FORUM ON FRANCHISING (1996)

Kathleen C. Anderson and Anthony M. Stiegler, *Put Muscle in Your Marks: Enforcing Intellectual Property Rights* W14, ABA FORUM ON FRANCHISING (1995)

Richard M. Asbill and Jane W. LaFranchi, *International Franchise Sales Laws—A Survey* W7, ABA FORUM ON FRANCHISING (2005)

Jeffery A. Brimer, Alison C. McElroy, and John Pratt, *Going International: What Additional Restraints Will You Face?* W4, ABA FORUM ON FRANCHISING (2011)

Michael G. Brennan, Alexander Konigsberg, and Philip F. Zeidman, *Globetrotting: A Workshop on International Franchising* 10/W8, ABA FORUM ON FRANCHISING (1994)

Michael G. Brennan, Alexander Konigsberg, and Philip F. Zeidman, *Globetrotting: Strategies for Launching U.S.*

Franchisors Abroad 2/P2, ABA FORUM ON FRANCHISING (1994)

Christopher P. Bussert and Jennifer Dolman, *Regaining Your Trademark After Abandonment or Misappropriation* W7, ABA FORUM ON FRANCHISING (2011)

Ronald T. Coleman and Linda K. Stevens, *Trade Secrets and Confidential Information: Rights and Remedies* W2, ABA FORUM ON FRANCHISING (2000)

Finola Cunningham, *Commerce Department Helps Franchisors Go Global*, in FRANCHISING WORLD 63 (Dec. 2005)

Michael R. Daigle and Alex S. Konigsberg, *Meeting Off-Shore Disclosure and Contract Requirements* F/W13, ABA FORUM ON FRANCHISING (1992)

Jennifer Dolman, Robert A. Lauer, and Lawrence M. Weinberg, Structuring International Master Franchise Relationships for Success and Responding When Things Go Awry W22, ABA FORUM ON FRANCHISING (2007)

Gary R. Duvall, Paul Jones, and Jane LaFranchi, *Planning for the International Enforcement of Franchise Agreements* W6, ABA FORUM ON FRANCHISING (1999)

William Edwards, International Expansion: Do Opportunities Outweigh Challenges? in FRANCHISING WORLD (February 2008)

George J. Eydt and Stuart Hershman, *Bringing a Foreign Franchise System to the United States* W9, ABA FORUM ON FRANCHISING (2009)

William A. Finkelstein and Louis T. Pirkey, *International Trademarks* W15, ABA FORUM ON FRANCHISING (1991)

William A. Finkelstein, Protecting Trademarks Internationally: Current Strategies and Developments B3, ABA FORUM ON FRANCHISING (1996)

Stephen Giles, Lou H. Jones, and Lawrence Weinberg, *Negotiating and Documenting Complex International Franchise Agreements* W21, ABA FORUM ON FRANCHISING (2006)

Steven M. Goldman, Stephen Giles, Marc Israel, and Stanley Wong, *Competition Round Up from Around the World* LB2, ABA FORUM ON FRANCHISING (2004)

David C. Gryce and E. Lynn Perry, *Trademarks and Copyrights in the International Arena* 6/W4, ABA FORUM ON FRANCHISING (1993)

Kenneth S. Kaplan, Andrew P. Loewinger, and Penelope J. Ward, *System Standards in International Franchising* W14, ABA FORUM ON FRANCHISING (2005)

Edward Levitt and Jorge Mondragon, A Survey of International Legal Traps and How to Avoid Them—Beyond the Franchise Laws W20, ABA FORUM ON FRANCHISING (2007)

Ned Levitt, Kendal H. Tyre, and Penny Ward, *The Impossible Dream: Controlling Your International Franchise System* W4, ABA FORUM ON FRANCHISING (2010)

Michael K. Lindsey and Andrew P. Loewinger, *International (Non-U.S.) Franchise Disclosure Requirements* W9, ABA FORUM ON FRANCHISING (2002)

Andrew P. Loewinger and John Pratt, *Recent Changes and Trends in International Franchise Laws* W4, ABA FORUM ON FRANCHISING (2008)

Andrew P. Loewinger and Thomas M. Pitegoff, Avoiding the Long Arm of the Law in International Franchising: Issues and Approaches W8, ABA FORUM ON FRANCHISING (1995)

Craig J. Madson and Katherine C. Spelman, *Similarity and Confusion in the Intellectual Property Arena* W11, ABA FORUM ON FRANCHISING (1997)

Christopher A. Nowak, John Pratt, and Carl E. Zwisler, *Franchising Internationally with Countries with Opaque Legal Systems* W20, ABA FORUM ON FRANCHISING (2006)

E. Lynn Perry and John L. Sullivan Jr., *Trademark Compliance and Enforcement Techniques* E/W12, ABA FORUM ON FRANCHISING (1992)

Marcel Portmann, *Franchising Sector Proves Global Reach*, in FRANCHISING WORLD (January 2007)

John Pratt and Luiz Henrique O. do Amaral, Civil Law for Common Law Practitioners (or How to Draft an Agreement for Use Overseas) W4, ABA FORUM ON FRANCHISING (2002)

Kirk W. Reilly, Robert F. Salkowski and Geoffrey B. Shaw, *Determining the Rules of Engagement in Litigation Here and Abroad* W5, ABA FORUM ON FRANCHISING (2008)

Catherine Riesterer and Frank Zaid, *Basics of International Franchising* L/B2, ABA FORUM ON FRANCHISING (1997)

W. Andrew Scott and Christopher N. Wormald, *Stranger in a Strange Land: Contrasting Franchising in International Expansion* W2, ABA FORUM ON FRANCHISING (2003)

Donald Smith and Erik Wulff, *International Franchising: The Unraveling of an International Franchise Relationship* 15/W13, ABA FORUM ON FRANCHISING (1993)

Frank Zaid, Pamela Mills, and Michael Santa Maria, *Essential Issues in International Franchising* LB/1, ABA FORUM ON FRANCHISING (2001)

II. Asian Resources

Stephen Giles, Andrew P. Loewinger, and Sherin Sakr, *Go East Young Franchisor: Franchising in Asia-Pacific Other Than China and India* W21, ABA FORUM ON FRANCHISING (2011)

Stephen Giles, *Franchising in Asia-Pacific Region, Who's Who Legal*: FRANCHISE 2012 (2012)

A. China

Ren Yanling, *Changes to Chinese Franchise Law: An improved Balance Between the Interests of Franchisors and Franchisees*, in INT'L JOURNAL OF FRANCHISING LAW 3 (2012)

China: New Franchsing Law, in Int'l Journal of FRANCHISING LAW 2 (2005)

Ella S.K. Cheong, *China*, in INTERNATIONAL FRANCHISING CHN/1 (Dennis Campbell gen. ed. 2011)

Yu Qin and Richard L. Wageman, *China*, in INTERNATIONAL FRANCHISE SALES LAWS China-1 (Andrew P. Loewinger and Michael K. Lindsey eds. 2010)

Mark Abell, Daniela C. Brito, and Paul D. Jones, *Franchising in the BRIC Markets (Brazil, Russia, India, and China)* W18, ABA FORUM ON FRANCHISING (2008)

B. Hong Kong

Andrea S.Y. Fong, *Hong Kong*, in INTERNATIONAL FRANCHISING HK/1 (Dennis Campbell gen. ed. 2011)

C. India

Preeti Mehta, *India—Termination of Master Franchise Agreements and the Consequences*, in INT'L JOURNAL OF FRANCHISING LAW 3 (2007)

Yoginder Pal, *Franchising in India*, FRANCHISING WORLD (October 2006)

Mark Abell, Daniela C. Brito and Paul D. Jones, *Franchising in the BRIC Markets (Brazil, Russia, India, and China)* W18, ABA FORUM ON FRANCHISING (2008)

D. Indonesia

Sigit Ardianto and Rivan F. Ramadhan, *Indonesia*, in INTERNATIONAL FRANCHISING INA/1 (Dennis Campbell gen. ed. 2011)

Rick Beckman and Ferry P. Madian, *Indonesia*, in INTERNATIONAL FRANCHISE SALES LAWS Indonesia-1 (Andrew P. Loewinger and Michael K. Lindsey eds. 2010)

Kendal H. Tyre, Jr. & Pierce Haesung Han, *The Ministry of Trade of Indonesia Limits Growth of Food and Beverage Franchises*, NIXON PEABODY LLP: FRANCHISE ALERT (February 2013)

E. Japan

Takenari Shimizu, *Japan*, in INTERNATIONAL FRANCHISING JAP/1 (Dennis Campbell gen. ed. 2011)

Souichirou Kozuka and Takashi Kanai, *Japan*, in INTERNATIONAL FRANCHISE SALES LAWS Japan-1 (Andrew P. Loewinger and Michael K. Lindsey eds. 2010)

F. Malaysia

Leela Baskaran, *Malaysia*, in INTERNATIONAL FRANCHISING MAY/1 (Dennis Campbell gen. ed. 2011)

Mohd Bustaman Hj Abdullah and Wong Sai Fong, *Malaysia*, in INTERNATIONAL FRANCHISE SALES LAWS Malaysia-1 (Andrew P. Loewinger and Michael K. Lindsey eds. 2010)

Kendal H. Tyre, Jr. & Pierce Haesung Han, *Malaysian Government Actively Promotes Growth in Franchise Sector*, NIXON PEABODY LLP: FRANCHISE ALERT (October 2013)

Kendal H. Tyre, Jr. & Pierce Haesung Han, *Tapping Into Malaysia's Aggressive Franchising Goals*, PORTFOLIO MEDIA, INC.: LAW360 (November 2013)

G. Singapore

Daniel Lim, Bernard Lui, Michele The, and Vanessa Chew, *Singapore*, in INTERNATIONAL FRANCHISING SIN/1 (Dennis Campbell gen. ed. 2011)

H. South Korea

Brendon Carr and Jae-Hoon Kim, *South Korea*, in INTERNATIONAL FRANCHISE SALES LAWS South Korea-1 (Andrew P. Loewinger and Michael K. Lindsey eds. 2010)

Kendal H. Tyre, Jr. & Pierce Haesung Han, *South Korea adopts major amendments to the Fair Transactions in Franchise Business Act*, NIXON PEABODY LLP: FRANCHISE LAW ALERT (January 2014)

I. Taiwan

Wellington Liu and David Lu, *Taiwan*, in INTERNATIONAL FRANCHISE SALES LAWS Taiwan-1 (Andrew P. Loewinger and Michael K. Lindsey eds. 2010)

J. Thailand

Alan Adcock and Sriwan Puapondh, *Thailand*, in INTERNATIONAL FRANCHISING THA/1 (Dennis Campbell gen. ed. 2011)

K. Vietnam

Mai Minh Hang and Nguyen Anh Tran, *Vietnam*, in INTERNATIONAL FRANCHISE SALES LAWS Vietnam-1 (Andrew P. Loewinger and Michael K. Lindsey eds. 2010)

Printed in Dunstable, United Kingdom

91343667R00030